"The recipe for a truly Catholic home is not easy to find. That's why a book like Sr. Kathleen's will be welcomed both by parents and religious educators. *Catholic Family, Catholic Home* contains prayers, activities, and projects, some familiar, some new, all based on our rich Catholic tradition. The reflection questions help families assess their own situation; the family projects includes ideas on hospitality (a lost art) and a family pledge of nonviolence; and the rituals and celebrations offer suggestions for birthdays, baptisms, anniversaries, reconciliation, and more. Sr. Kathleen deserves a round of applause!"

Alison Berger
Author, Editor of *Religion Teacher's Journal*

"*Catholic Family, Catholic Home* is a great resource for any family, but especially valuable for parents who want to pass on their Catholic faith and aren't sure where to begin. It helps families get in touch with the liturgical year, and is an excellent guide for strengthening and enriching families in their faith journey."

Kay and Gary Aitchison
Executive Directors, Christian Family Movement

"Sr. Kathleen here shares time-tested, unique, and creative ways to live our Catholic faith. This book prompted me to ask myself 'How do we make conscious choices to invite Christ and God into our home?' and 'How do we welcome friends, extended family, and others into our home?' The answers come by way of ideas for creating a Catholic atmosphere in the home, celebrations and rituals, seasonal family projects, and activities to unite and strengthen the family. The final pages of the book feature the author's favorite Catholic family prayers."

Lisa M. Coleman
Co-author, *Basics of the Catholic Faith*

"This book has all the stuff that keeps a Catholic family spiritually alive and well. The activities are timeless, fun, and easy to do; the prayers are simple and heartfelt. I have already tried at least five of the book's suggestions with my family, and we all look forward to trying the rest! *Catholic Fam~~ily, Catholic Home~~* is a ~~r~~eal joy for nurturing faith at home."

Mary Carol Kendzia
~~Edit~~or, *Lent for Families: A Time to Grow*

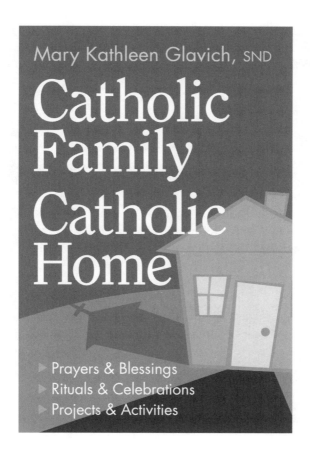

Mary Kathleen Glavich, SND

Catholic Family Catholic Home

- Prayers & Blessings
- Rituals & Celebrations
- Projects & Activities

TWENTY-THIRD PUBLICATIONS
BAYARD ⊕ Mystic, CT 06355

Acknowledgments

My gratitude to Marcia Stobierski, Marianna Gattozi, Nancy Dill, and Linda Hildebrand, who graciously shared their family experiences with me and acted as consultants for this book. Also thank you to Claudette Matero-Bolce for her support and assistance.

Vocation Prayer for Families found on page 18 used with permission of the Diocesan Vocation Office of the Diocese of Cleveland, Ohio.

Father's Day Prayer found on pages 18 and 19 used with permission from the Department for Marriage and Family Ministry of the Diocese of Cleveland, Ohio. May be reprinted.

The Family Pledge for Nonviolence found on pp. 33-34 is used with permission from the Families Against Violence Advocacy Network (FAVAN) of the Institute for Peace and Justice (www.hometown.aol.com/ppjn/favan.html).

The Scripture passages contained herein are from the *New Revised Standard Version of the Bible*, copyright © 1989, by the Division of Christian Education of the National Council of Churches of Christ in the U.S.A. All rights reserved.

Twenty-Third Publications/ Bayard
185 Willow Street
P.O. Box 180
Mystic, CT 06355
(860) 536-2611
(800) 321-0411

ISBN:1-58595-118-8
Library of Congress Catalog Card Number: 00-134899
Printed in the U.S.A.

Dedication

To my family:
Mom, Dad, Nancy, Buddy, Ted, Andy,
Marcia, Tom, Tommy, Kathleen, Julie,
Lisa, Anthony, Sabina, and Arline

Contents

Introduction

Where did you learn about the Mass? The story of Christmas? To say the Our Father and Hail Mary? That you should share your toys with others? That hitting someone is wrong? If you're like most people, your answer to all of these questions is "at home." And you can probably identify with the boy who, when asked, "Why do you believe in God?" said, "I guess it's just something that runs in our family." We may smile at this answer, but if we reflect on it, the child was right. For the vast majority of people, faith is something acquired from the family.

The faith of saints like Thérèse of Lisieux was forged in the heart of their families. Likewise, Mary and Joseph nurtured the faith of Jesus, the God-Man. Even if you did not come from a particularly holy family, chances are your faith began and was fostered at home.

The impact of one's family on religious and moral formation far outweighs the impact of even the best Catholic school. Most children today spend thirty hours in religion class during the course of one year. If they attend Catholic school, they are in religion class approximately ninety hours a year. In contrast to this, subtracting the time children are sleeping and at school, they are at home under the influence of their families about 4,903 hours a year! Consider too that during the first five years of a child's life—which psychologists tell us are the most formative years—the child is not in religion class at all unless he or she attends a religion-based preschool.

More than ever we are recognizing that the basic cell of the church is not the parish church building—but the home. Parents* are the first teachers of their children. You tell your children the good news of God's love and show them the love of God before anyone else does. Through you, they become aware that they are called to a special relationship with God and learn how to come in touch with God through prayer. In the circle of your family your children discover how to live

1

Christ's way of love. The family is actually the school of Christian life. Several church documents underline the role of parents in passing on the faith to their children:

> The family, so to speak, is the domestic church. In it parents should, by their word and example, be the first preachers of the faith to their children.
>
> —*Dogmatic Constitution on the Church, #11*

> Family catechesis precedes, accompanies, and enriches other forms of instruction in the faith.
>
> —*Catechism of the Catholic Church, #2226*

> Parents must be acknowledged as the first and foremost educators of their children. Their role as educators is so decisive that scarcely anything can compensate for their failure in it. For it confers on parents to create a family atmosphere so animated with love and reverence for God and others that a well-rounded personal and social development will be fostered among the children.... Let parents, then, clearly recognize how vital a truly Christian family is for the life and development of God's own people.
>
> —*Declaration on Christian Education, #3*

As much as you may wish to nurture the faith of your children at home, you may not know how to go about it. In addition, work situations and other pressing matters may prevent you from devising ways to practice the faith in your family. In this book, you will find numerous suggestions for living the faith at home and questions for reflection at the end of each chapter to spark your thoughts. For more ideas, talk with other parents, locate Christian magazines and books similar to this one, and search the Internet using words like "family faith," "Catholic families," and "Christmas customs." No doubt, you will add your own personal touches to the activities and come up with original ideas.

The structure, character, and schedule of your family life may automatically veto some of the ideas proposed here for family faith. Do not lose heart! Each family has its unique style of life and traditions. Families have different compositions and members of different ages. Some have younger children, others have teenagers. Some have one parent, others include grandparents. Adopt the practices that are feasible and comfortable for your family. Occasionally dare to try something that you think might not work. The Spirit moves in strange and surprising ways!

Persevere. Be strong-willed enough to initiate and keep up some of the Catholic practices suggested here. Something the children complain about or make fun of at first may become a treasured memory for them someday. You may even find them continuing certain practices when they have families of their own.

May all your efforts help make your family another holy family, one that truly is the domestic church.

*In this book, the term "parents" is intended to include guardians and anyone who is a caretaker of the children at home.

1
Living the Faith

While I was out working in the yard recently, a priest drove up the driveway. He said he was the brother of the woman who used to live in our house. She and her husband, both deceased, had raised five girls there. Each girl now worked for the church in some capacity. The priest said that every once in a while he deliberately drove past the house, explaining wistfully, "It was a house of love."

Catholic images, prayers, and rituals alone do not make a Catholic home. Over and above these things, the family must live the faith and radiate love in keeping with Christ's commandments, beatitudes, and example. What is more important: to have a crucifix in every room or to accept trials with trust in God? To say meal prayers routinely or to share food with the hungry? To display a bumper sticker that asks, "What would Jesus do?" or to be a courteous driver? The answers are obvious. In the eyes of Jesus, who chastised the hypocritical Pharisees for their show of righteousness, outward piety can't compare with integrity, unselfishness, and love in practice.

Children who constantly see and share in their parents' faith have a better chance of growing up Catholic. What is important to parents becomes important to their children. If you value taking care of your health, your children will learn to care for their own. If you regard all people as equal and deserving of respect, so will your children. If you speak well of priests and religious and occasionally invite them to dinner or to a family activity, your children will develop an appreciation for people dedicated to God. Your children might even entertain the idea that God may be calling them to a special life of service in the church. If you take an active role in your parish's RCIA program or attempt to share your faith with a neighbor who has none, your children will learn to cherish their Catholic heritage.

Another powerful way to foster faith is to associate with other people of faith. Spending time with other families of believers can be a great support to your efforts to live the Christian life. Similarly, you'll want to guide your children toward friends whose values align with your own. As you probably know, the friends of your children have influence over them that is only surpassed by yours—and at times supersedes yours.

Christian Choices

Your children are growing up bombarded by practices that are contrary to the way of life Jesus teaches. In the media and in their neighborhood they see all kinds of behavior. You must teach them that just because a practice is prevalent doesn't make it right. What seems normal can actually be an aberration that keeps us from being the fully alive and loving people God intends us to be. Handing on Christian values to your children is a challenge and a real battle.

Basically, you transmit your attitudes and values to your children by the choices you make every day. (Hopefully, through prayer and grace you will not be sending them conflicting messages!) From you they can learn to look at God and then choose. Some examples of choices that form your children into Christians are:

- going to Mass and actively participating
- refraining from getting back at a neighbor
- being frugal with water, electricity, and paper
- telling the truth even when it's difficult
- avoiding objectionable movies
- subscribing to a Catholic periodical
- apologizing
- welcoming foreigners
- looking to God for help when trouble comes
- respecting life
- donating money and time to your parish
- helping someone in trouble

Besides learning a Catholic lifestyle by osmosis, children can be directly taught it. This can be done in seven ways:

1. Tell your children what Catholics believe and do, and explain why. Have the patience to state things a hundred times. Many repetitions may be necessary for the concepts to take hold. Teach your children to make the Sign of the Cross as a symbol of their faith in the Trinity and the saving acts of Jesus. Teach them to realize that Easter is more than candy and the Easter bunny, that it is the celebration of Christ's resurrection and a promise of our own. Teach them to care for the poor and needy as they would care for Christ himself because Jesus told us that anything done for the least of his brothers and sisters he sees as done to him.

2. Take time to answer your children's questions about religion thoughtfully and thoroughly. This will help keep the lines of communication open in the future. Questions like "What is heaven like?" and "Can I believe in reincarnation?" might require some research on your part.

3. When a family decision is made, spell out for your children the values that determined it. These decisions range from crucial ones like deciding on a new home to mundane ones like deciding what to watch on television.

4. Don't just forbid your children to do something, but explain why you are forbidding it. Tell them why you won't let them buy Pokemon cards, why you won't allow them go to a certain party, and why you don't want them to smoke.

5. Take advantage of issues that arise in the news, in a movie, or in life by discussing how a Christian would regard them. For instance, suppose some seniors at a local high school vandalize the school building and the principal cancels the prom. Discuss the morality of the actions of the students, the justice of the principal's reaction, and what could be done about the situation. Conversations like these can be held at the dinner table or in the car as you chauffeur your children to and from their activities.

6. Take an interest in your children's formal religious education. Ask

them what their religion lessons were about; help them do their homework. Better yet, volunteer to assist with the classes. At home, carry on the traditions your children see at the parish school. This will reinforce them.

7. Make sure your children understand in which ways their heroes are to be imitated and in which ways they are not. Point out good Christian models you see in the media and in your immediate circle of friends and family.

Finally, take heart in knowing that in much of your ordinary life you are passing on the gospel to your children without realizing it. Every time you scold your children for arguing or fighting, every time you encourage your children to share their candy, every time you insist on your children writing a thank-you note, you are enforcing Christ's commandment, "Love one another." You are creating a Catholic home.

FOR REFLECTION

- What family practices do you have that teach your children to be Christian?
- How have you transmitted gospel values to your children this week without deliberately intending to?
- What current events are opportunities for deepening your children's faith today?
- How do your friends and your children's friends strengthen or weaken your faith?

2

A Catholic Atmosphere

A father thought his three-year-old son was playing too quietly with the trains in his room. The man peeked in the room just in time to see the boy get up, run to the statue of the Sacred Heart, and kiss it. "Why did you do that?" the father asked. The boy replied, "Because he's a good guy." Obviously the child knew a basic tenet of faith, reinforced by a visual the family used to nurture their spiritual life.

Religious Objects

It's a good idea for Catholics to decorate their homes with a few reminders of God. Your house doesn't have to resemble a religious goods store, but there should be some objects that foster faith. These are most effective and inspiring if they are in good taste and not saccharine depictions. The *Catechism of the Catholic Church* says of sacramentals, "by the Church's prayer, they prepare us to receive grace and dispose us to cooperate with it" (#1670). Do visitors see any of the following objects in your home?

- a crucifix (a traditional one, one showing a resurrected Christ, or a brightly painted one from Latin America)

- a statue or picture of Jesus (e.g., the Sacred Heart, the Infant of Prague, the Good Shepherd)

- an image of Mary

- an image of St. Joseph, St. Thérèse of Lisieux, St. Anthony, or another saint

- an image of a church hero such as the Pope John Paul II, the four women martyred in El Salvador, Dorothy Day, or Bishop Oscar Romero

- an icon, such as Rublev's "The Trinity," "Our Lady of Perpetual

Help," or modern icons of Jesus and the saints

- a religious masterpiece or the depiction of a Scripture event
- a vigil light before the image of Jesus or a saint
- an image of an angel
- a relic of a saint
- plaques with religious sayings printed, painted, or in needlework
- a religious poster or plaque
- palm (plain, braided, or formed into a cross)
- a Catholic calendar
- incense
- an *ojo de Dios* (eye of God)
- an object (mug, magnet, key chain, paperweight, etc.) with a religious theme
- a holy water container, perhaps water from the Holy Land or Lourdes
- a blessed candle
- the Bible
- religious books, periodicals, videos, or games

Objects can keep you mindful of the mysteries of the church year. For example, use an Advent wreath or Easter eggs as the centerpiece on the dining room table or as the decoration on the mantel. During May, in honor of Mary, set up a May altar with fresh flowers around it. For Christmas, in addition to Santa, elves, and lighted icicles, make a nativity scene part of your indoor and/or outdoor decorations. For Easter, hang eggs on a tree and display a large Easter flag. Keep a family bulletin board (designed to correspond to the seasons and feasts of the church year).

Jewish people fasten a *mezuzah* to their doorways. This is a small box that contains Scripture verses that are key to the Jewish faith. The family members touch it reverently as they come and go. A parallel Catholic custom is to have a holy water font at the doorways as a reminder of baptism. We bless ourselves with the water just as we do at the entrance of our churches. Holy water, which is blessed at the

Easter Vigil, is available from your parish church. A container of it can be used for blessings in the home. Instead of a holy water font at your door, you might display a framed verse or prayer such as "Lord, bless all who pass through this door," or "Lord, bless our comings and our goings." Or you might wish to have a doorknob hanger with a religious saying, such as those designed to celebrate the millennium.

Another traditional custom is to own a blessed candle which is lit during storms, illnesses, and times of special needs. Candles are blessed in church on February 2, the feast of the Presentation, formerly called Candlemas Day. Candles are received at baptisms, weddings, and certain liturgical services. You can incorporate these church candles or beautiful decorative and scented candles into family prayer services and rituals.

You might extend your faith to your car or van by keeping a St. Christopher medal, a Sacred Heart statue or plaque, or a rosary in it. Your vehicle might sport a religious bumper sticker or decal. Let your faith overflow into your yard by means of a shrine or a statue of Mary or St. Francis of Assisi. Signs of faith not only touch our own hearts but witness our faith to others.

A Prayer Corner

Byzantine Catholics are proud to have a prayer corner in their homes. For them, this is a wall with icons (pictures) of the Mother of God and the patron saints of the family members. Family members bow to the icons and kiss them. Above the icons is a cross. On a table in front of the icons are a Bible, other blessed items such as holy water and palm, and a tray of sand for holding tapers. Hanging nearby is a lamp with a candle that is kept burning. A censer (for burning incense during prayer) is also on the table. On Saturday evening the father may carry the censer through the house, in blessing, to herald the beginning of the Lord's Day. The family gathers at their icon corner at significant moments in their lives such as the announcing of an engagement or a new job.

Consider setting up a simple prayer corner in your house and using it as the focus of family prayer. Choose a table, a dresser, the top of a bookcase, or a mantel and cover it with a decorative cloth. Place the family Bible, a crucifix, a candle, and perhaps a plant or flowers there. As the church year unfolds display palms, a nativity scene, an image of the saint of the day, or lenten reminders at your prayer corner. For Christmas set a poinsettia there; for Easter, a lily. You might also vary the cloth according to the liturgical season or feast day. Your children will enjoy decorating your family prayer corner with you and changing it from season to season.

The Bible

Sacred Scripture deserves a prominent place in a Catholic home. The Bible is not meant to be hidden away and taken out only to record births, weddings, and deaths. Rather, the Bible is to be used and displayed, if not at a prayer corner, then in another place of honor. Place a candle near it as a sign that Scripture is light for our lives. Purchase or make a beautiful cover to show respect and love for your Bible.

Give a Bible as a gift to someone, not only to celebrate a baptism, first communion, or confirmation, but for birthdays and weddings too. This will make a statement to your children and let them know that you value God's Word.

Post Scripture verses in your home, especially during special liturgical seasons. A family member might letter them by hand or design them on the computer. Discuss the verses and pray them.

FOR REFLECTION

- Mentally go through your home. What signs are there that it is the home of a Catholic family?

- What religious articles would you like to add to your house?

- Where could you set up a prayer corner in your house?

- Do you own a family Bible? If not, what steps could you take to obtain one?

- Where could you keep the Bible in your home so that it is honored and accessible?

3

Family Prayer and Blessings

The father of a family who lived in the country spent all night driving a snowplow. Suddenly, at 6:00 a.m., he felt as though he had had a strong cup of coffee. He was reinvigorated. Why? Because he knew that at that time his wife and children were praying for him at breakfast. Family members who pray with and for one another enjoy a strength that other families do not.

Prayer Customs

What if your family has never prayed together before? How do you get started? It is preferable and easier to begin praying together when children are little; however, better late than never. Parents are usually the ones who at first feel uncomfortable and self-conscious praying together. To the children, praying is natural. Customs and rituals of prayer can be introduced gradually, one at a time, beginning with night prayers. Don't expect to transform your family into a monastic community all at once!

Some prayer customs take little time at all. It's just a matter of remembering to do them and making them a habit. Here are some ways to incorporate prayer into family life.

- *Night prayers.* These will vary with the age of the children. The children may pray informally, thanking God for the day and asking forgiveness for wrongdoing. They may ask God to bless certain people as well as their pet. Formal prayers such as an Our Father, a Hail Mary, or an Act of Contrition can be added. It helps to have the children kneel next to their bed for night prayers. To make a lasting impression, kneel and pray with them. When the children are older, consider praying Night Prayer from the Liturgy of the Hours, the church's official prayer.

- *Prayer before and after meals.* Granted, for many busy modern families a meal together at table is a rare event. If and when your family eats together, remember the Giver of all food. Pray the traditional grace, "Bless us, O Lord, and these thy gifts..." or a different version. There are simple poems and songs that are meal prayers, including the somewhat flippant cheer: "Rub-a-dub-dub, Thanks for the grub. Yeah God!" You might collect meal prayers and keep them in a box on the table. Incidentally, one of the best meal prayers is the Our Father. During grace, you might ask God to bless those who supplied and prepared the food and pray that the hungry who lack such good meals may be fed. One variation of prayer before meals is to invite each person to mention something he or she would like to give thanks for. As grace is prayed, you might hold hands or put your arms around one another's shoulders. Make it a point to say meal prayers together.

- *Prayers in need.* Let each family member choose an object to represent him or her. Whenever a person is in need of special prayer, he or she places this object at the prayer corner to alert the rest of the family to his or her personal need.

- *Creative prayer times.* Find your own times to pray together. One mother I know prays with her son in the car on the way to school every day.

Spontaneous Prayers

Teach your children to say spontaneous prayers as freely as they say, "God bless you" when someone sneezes. By doing this they will realize that God is with us every day of our lives, not just on Sundays.

- When your family witnesses a beautiful landscape, a spectacular sunset, or enjoys an experience such as swimming in a lake on a hot day, say a prayer of praise.

- When something wonderful happens, say a short prayer of thanksgiving.

- When a tragic event is in the news, pray for the victims.

- When you hear a siren, pray for anyone in danger.

- When you pass a homeless person or someone begging on the street, pray for him or her.

- When you pass a farm while driving or see loaded shelves in a supermarket, say a prayer of gratitude to God for food.

- When you travel past a cemetery, pray, "Eternal rest grant unto them, O Lord, and let perpetual light shine upon them. May they rest in peace. Amen."

- Teach small children psalm verses, in particular those from the responsorial psalms at Mass. For example, in times of joy they can exclaim, "Bless the Lord, my soul, and all that is within me bless his holy name" (Psalm 103:1). When they are frightened they can say, "Guard me as the apple of the eye; hide me in the shadow of your wings" (Psalm 17:8–9).

Family Prayer Times

Father Patrick Peyton's slogan, "The family that prays together, stays together" is still true. United in prayer, your family members are more likely to have a stronger love for and commitment to one another. By being mindful of God and calling on God together, you will not only grow personally, you become a powerhouse of good for society.

You might ask, "But how can our family manage to pray together when there's barely even time to eat together?" Usually there is always time to do the things you really want to do. Families who are convinced that prayer together is important make time to do it. Soon it becomes a habit.

Set aside a specific time and place to pray together. You might want to have each member sign a contract agreeing to be present and to schedule other things around this family prayer time. If someone must be absent, set out his or her photo as a reminder of spiritual union in your family prayer. Let family members take turns leading the prayer time. This will result in an interesting variety.

Special occasions are good times for family prayer. For example, on

Christmas Eve plan a prayer service that includes the reading of the nativity story from the gospel of Luke.

There is no perfect way to pray together. Each family will find its own way. Don't be surprised if this aspect of family life is as human and as complicated as other aspects.

Blessings

A blessing is a prayer to call down God's goodness and protection on someone or something. The Catechism states, "Every baptized person is called to be a blessing and to bless" (#1669). You don't have to wear a roman collar to bless.

A friend of mine who has three daughters blesses them before they go to bed at night. He traces the Sign of the Cross on each of their foreheads and says simply, "May God bless you, in the name of the Father, and of the Son, and of the Holy Spirit." With the youngest girl, he began having her bless him too as he kneels. Now my friend wishes he had thought of this practice when the older girls were young.

Feel free to compose your own form of night blessing. One mother I know prays, "May the Lord bless you with peace and wake you with joy in the morning." You might compose a personal blessing for each child.

There are several ways to bestow a blessing: place both hands on the person's head, place a hand on each side of the person's face, trace a cross on the person, or give him or her a warm hug. To make a blessing special, use holy water or holy oil.

Give blessings before the children leave home for the day, on a special occasion, for a birthday, for a baptismal anniversary, and for a name day. Make up your own words or use a book like *Catholic Household Blessings and Prayers*. Published by the United States Catholic Conference, this book is a treasury of blessings for families for special days and moments in the life of the family. These are some of those blessings:

Blessing for a family

Blessing on birthdays or the anniversary of baptism

Blessings before and after birth

Blessing for times of sickness

Blessing for times of trouble

Blessing for times of new beginnings

Blessing of parents after a miscarriage

Blessing before leaving on a journey

Blessing before moving from a home

Blessing of tools for work

Blessing of objects for use or entertainment

Blessing of fields and gardens

Blessing of animals

Blessing of a Christmas tree

Special Prayers

If you do not already pray the rosary together, your family might begin the custom. Pray at least a decade a day. This well-loved prayer not only honors the Mother of God but also puts the life of Jesus before you as you meditate on the mysteries.

To be in tune with the world's current fascination with angels, but more than that, to teach the children to turn to these special friends and protectors for help and comfort, say the Guardian Angel Prayer. A modern version that is easier for children to understand than the traditional version is found on page 68.

Your family might say a traveling prayer before going on a car trip together. You might invoke St. Raphael, St. Christopher, your guardian angels, and your family patron saints to keep you safe on the road.

Two longstanding Catholic prayer traditions are *novenas* (nine days of prayer) and *triduums* (three days of prayer). Your family might make a novena or a triduum before a special feast or before a family member celebrates a sacrament. For instance, on the three days before the feast of the Immaculate Conception you might pray a Hail Mary at dinner.

A Catholic custom that you might introduce to your children is bowing your head whenever the name of Jesus is mentioned.

If your parish has eucharistic adoration, consider signing up for an hour (or a shorter time) as a family. Guide your children in using this time well by giving them prayerbooks or ideas for prayer.

Sung Prayers

Teach the children religious songs: hymns, songs for children by modern composers, and camp songs like "This Little Light of Mine" and "Joshua Fought the Battle of Jericho." Your children will be singing these just the way we find ourselves singing songs from commercials or the top ten list. They will sing them in the bathtub and in the car. At the same time, they will be growing in faith. If you have older children, introduce them to today's good Christian music produced especially for teens and young adults. Also, teach them the Taizé way of praying in which one line is chanted over and over.

During family meals or on long car trips you might play a recording of Christian music, such as Gregorian chant.

Reading Scripture

We believe that Scripture is God's Word to us. In it, we find guidance for our lives. Through it, we come to meet God and to understand God's great love for us. Young children can become familiar with God's stories if along with the usual fairy tales you tell them Bible stories. Moreover, a lifelong habit can be formed when your family has the custom of reading the Bible together for five minutes every day, perhaps at the end of dinner. A simple translation of the Bible for families is the Contemporary English Version. Of course, children favor Bibles that have colorful illustrations.

Besides reading the Bible regularly, your family might also try to prepare for the Sunday readings (at least the gospel readings) together the day before. (Often, the citations for the readings of the coming Sunday are given in the parish bulletin. Or you can ask the parish staff or a Christian bookstore to recommend a resource that gives the readings for each Sunday of the year.) Read the passage, discuss its meaning, and then talk about what it means for you personally. After Mass, you can discuss the readings and the homily on the way home or at a meal together.

The psalms are the church's daily prayers. Make appropriate psalms part of your family prayer on different occasions. Certain ones make good morning prayers (Psalms 5:1–8; 90:12–17, 108:2–7), meal prayers (Psalms 23:5–6, 104:13–15, 145:15–18), and evening prayers

(Psalms 51, 96, 103:1–5).

To make God's Word more a part of your life, your family might memorize Bible verses together and play games with them. For instance, make a jigsaw puzzle out of the words and race to see who can assemble it the fastest. Memorizing psalm verses encourages prayer. They will also come readily to mind when they are needed.

A moving way to read Scripture is in the dark by the light of a candle. Give everyone a verse to read. Pass the candle carefully from one reader to the next.

Prepared Prayers

Make use of family prayers and prayer services that you find in magazines or parish bulletins. Here are two examples:

Vocation Prayer for Families

Christ Jesus, you became a human person to teach us how to love. It was in a human family where you grew in wisdom, age, and grace. Our family is the place where we first come to know God, and to learn who we are. Family is the place where we, took, grow in wisdom, age, and grace.

Give our family the gifts of your Spirit. Help us to enjoy each other in the good times, to support each other through the difficult times, and to see your presence in each other all the time.

Help us to always bring out the best in each other—encourage each person in our family to use his or her gifts and talents fully. May we always help each other to be open to who you call us to be. As we grow in wisdom, age, and grace, may we always respond to your call to holiness, wherever that path may lead: in marriage, single life, ordained priesthood, or vowed religious life. Amen.

—Sister Mary Rose Kocab, SIW

Father's Day

Families may pray the following prayer and blessing for fathers or grandfathers, adapting the prayer as needed. Adapt the prayer to be used for mothers and grandmothers.

The family gathers for a meal. A candle may be lit. A favorite hymn may be sung.

Father: We begin in the name of the Father † , and of the Son, and of the Holy Spirit. Let us pray. Heavenly Father, guide us by your Word and sustain us in your love as we grow as a Christian family.

Scripture is read, such as Ephesians 6:1–4.
Reflections may be shared, after the reading.

Father: On this father's day, I commit myself to love and honor you, my family. I promise to provide for, protect, and guide you to the best of my abilities. I pray for God's wisdom, love, and strength to help me be the best father I can be.

The whole family or one member prays the following prayer as the family holds hands or places their hands on the father:

God our creator, in your wisdom and love you made all things. You made us and call us to grow in your love as a Christian family. Thank you for our father in this family. Strengthen and encourage him with your strength and wisdom. Let the example of his faith and love shine forth. Grant that we, his family, may honor him always with a spirit of gratitude. Grant this through Christ our Lord. Amen.

All pray the Lord's Prayer and share a sign of peace.
All share in the meal.

FOR REFLECTION

- Do you ever say meal prayers or night prayers together? If not, how can you introduce them?

- How can your family begin to have a regular family prayer time?

- What would be occasions for your family members to receive blessings?

- Do your children know that you pray?

- What message does Psalm 128 have for you?

4

Rituals and Celebrations

Every Christmas morning my sister takes a picture of her two boys coming down the stairs to the tree. The boys are now in their twenties, and they still go through this ritual!

Rituals are celebrations during which truth can sink into our hearts. Rituals offer ways to express feelings, teach lessons, make memories, heal, and cause joy. Rituals also link the past to the future. Through them, we understand who we are, where we've been, and where we're going. They establish a family identity. Some rituals are natural, everyday practices like the way we greet each other in the morning and the way we say goodnight. There are also family rituals for marking special events—for instance, the way we celebrate Christmas or birthdays. Rituals can also communicate Catholic identity from one generation to the next. New rituals for bonding a family together can always be adopted. Here are a few ideas for family rituals.

Family Candle   Make a Christ candle to light on festive occasions. Purchase a large candle and decorate it with a symbol for Christ. Or if you are more ambitious, make a tin lantern. Clean a tin can thoroughly. Fill the can with water and put it in the freezer. When the water is frozen, draw a design on the can with a marker. (Or draw it on paper and fasten the paper to the can with rubber bands.) Lay the can on its side on newspapers or thick cloths and, using a hammer and nails of various sizes, pierce the can along the design. This will make a pattern of holes which will emit light when a candle inside is lit. Once the ice is melted, put a candle in the can. When the candle is lit, make sure the hot can is on a trivet or something that will not be damaged by heat.

Keep the Christ candle in your prayer corner. Set it in a centerpiece of flowers or leaves on your table on days such as baptismal anniversaries, Easter, Christmas, or Candlemas Day (February 2).

Family Cup Purchase or make a family blessing cup to be used on special occasions as a symbol of shared life and love. Let each family member participate in choosing or making the cup. Bless the cup and say a prayer asking God to use it to pour out graces on your family and increase its love. Then use the cup whenever your family has a special meal. Before the meal, fill the cup with a drink. Read a Scripture passage that is related to the occasion and pray petitions asking for certain blessings. Pass the cup around the table for all to share. Close the ritual with a prayer such as the Our Father.

Firsts Celebrate "firsts" with rituals and prayers: a first tooth, a first raise, learning to ride a bike, the first day of school, the first date, a first game, and so on.

Setting a Place for Christ On Sundays and special feasts set a place at the table for Christ. He may come as a stranger, a passerby, or an unexpected family member. When the extra place is not filled, it will remind you of the Lord's presence.

Family Meetings Hold meetings regularly during which family members can solve problems and reach decisions cooperatively. Begin the meeting with a prayer and end it with a snack. During these meetings plan ways to be a vibrant Christian family. Books are available that provide ideas for family meetings. One is *Make Family Time Prime Time* by Denise Yribarren and DeAnn Koestner, Twenty-Third Publications.

Celebrating Birthdays

Remember God, the source of life, in celebrating birthdays. Here are several ideas for celebrating:

• Ask everyone at the party or at dinner to say a short prayer for the person who is celebrating the gift of life.

• Invite everyone to express a birthday wish for the person.

• Read a Scripture passage about life, such as Psalm 139.

• Have everyone mention how the person has brought God's love to the family.

• Go to Mass together and pray for the intentions of the person who has a birthday.

- Display a special birthday flag or banner for the person.
- Look up the exact time of the person's birth and, if possible, observe a few moments of silence and prayer at that time thanking God for the gift of life.

Celebrating Baptisms

When we were baptized, we were born into new, eternal life. Why not celebrate the day of family members' baptisms just as we celebrate our birthday? Here are some ways to do this:

- On the anniversary of the baptism let the child select his or her favorite meal.
- Provide water or flavored water to drink as a way of remembering the water used at baptism.
- Celebrate Eucharist together, as a family, for the child.
- Invite the godparents and the person who baptized the child to a special meal or party. If the godparents can't be present, ask them to write a letter to the child.
- Display photos and articles from the baptism (the baptismal certificate, the white garment, candle, greeting cards).
- Tell the story of the baptism.
- Tell how and why the child received his or her name.
- Light the baptismal candle and have the child renew the baptismal vows.
- Serve a decorated cake and ice cream.
- Give the child gifts, especially those that will help him or her live the faith.
- Have the parents and godparents renew their commitment to the child.
- Help the child make a commitment to Christ.

Celebrating Namedays

Family members who have a saint's name can celebrate the feast of that saint. Those who are not named for a particular saint might choose a saint as a patron and celebrate that saint's feast day. If your family has adopted a patron saint, celebrate that saint's feast day. Here are several ways to celebrate:

- Allow the person to enjoy a special meal on that day or choose a favorite activity for the family.
- Present the person with gifts, including one with the person's name on it.
- Display the picture or statue of the saint.
- Tell or read the story of the saint's life.
- Have other family members point out how the celebrating person resembles his or her namesake.
- Include a special prayer or blessing in the celebration.
- Tell the meaning of the name if possible. For example, Amy means beloved, and Douglas means seeker of light.
- Be creative in planning decorations and other ways to observe the feast. For example, if a child's name is Peter, rock candy would be an appropriate treat.

Celebrating a Wedding Anniversary

Keeping in mind that the union and love of the two people are signs of God's love for us, your whole family can celebrate a couple's wedding anniversary. The celebrating couple may be the father and mother, grandparents, aunts and uncles, or children. Here are some suggestions for a celebration ritual:

- The couple renews their wedding promises.
- Place the wedding rings in a small dish or bowl. During the celebration the husband and wife put them on each other again.
- Play a love song, perhaps "their song."
- Display the wedding pictures or show the video of the wedding.
- Pray for the couple. As part of the prayer service, read the story about the wedding of Cana from Scripture in John 2:1–11.

• Present the couple with a homemade card that incorporates a religious symbol and a prayer.

Celebrating Reconciliation

Most accidents happen in the home. Probably most sins occur in the home too. Children learn to seek forgiveness and to forgive in the family circle. Encourage your child to say "I'm sorry," and be quick to say it yourself to family members. Also, lead your child to learn how to make up for a wrongdoing.

In some families, it was the custom that before going to confession the children asked pardon of their parents for anything they had done wrong. You might plan a family reconciliation ritual in which members acknowledge their faults, say they are sorry, and extend forgiveness to others. This is a beautiful way to restore peace in the family.

A Family Reconciliation Service

The family members sit or stand in a circle.

Read a Scripture passage about our call to love such as John 15:12–17, 1 John 1:5—2:2, or 1 John 3:18–24.

After a period of reflection, family members ask forgiveness for times they have failed to love. This may be in the form of general petitions about faults and sins that hurt the family: "For the times we were late, forgive our selfishness," "For the times we were crabby, forgiven our selfishness."

Give forgiveness to one another verbally or through hugs.

Pray "Lord, Jesus Christ, Son of the living God, have mercy on me, a sinner."

Bless the children by making a Sign of the Cross on their foreheads.

Pray the Our Father holding hands.

Variations:
• Family members write faults on slips of paper. Crumple them up and burn them in a fireproof dish or throw them away. Then on other slips of paper write ways you intend to improve. Keep these slips as reminders of your resolutions.

• A parent prays a simple litany and the children repeat each line.

For the times I was impatient this week, forgive me, Lord.

For the times I was selfish this week, forgive me, Lord.

Then anyone may add anything in particular he or she regrets.

• Sing or listen to a song such as "Peace Is Flowing like a River."

Celebrating the Sacrament

Go to church to celebrate the sacrament of reconciliation together. On the day you are to go, hang a paper dove in the dining room as a reminder of the peace experienced from forgiveness. Before leaving for church, read a suitable Scripture passage such as those listed below. During the sacrament, pray for one another. Afterwards celebrate by going to an ice cream parlor or a pizza restaurant.

Scripture:
The lost sheep (Luke 15:1–7)
The lost coin (Luke 15:8–10)
The prodigal son (Luke 15:11–32)
The paralytic (Luke 5:17–26)
The forgiven woman (Luke 7:36–50)
Jesus and sinners (Matthew 9:9–13)
The gift of peace (John 20:19–23)

Celebrating Sundays

The third commandment is "Remember to keep holy the Lord's Day." Sunday, the Lord's Day, is meant to be different from the other six days of the week. Theologian Heather Murray Elkins speaks of the sabbath as a day for "altaring time." We observe the Lord's Day by praying, by celebrating the Eucharist, and by avoiding unnecessary work. One of the strongest ways to reinforce the message that the sabbath is a holy day is to try to go to Mass as a family each week.

Sunday should be a day of joy and rest, a chance for family members to interact, communicate, and become more united. In 1998 Pope John Paul II wrote a letter called "The Day of the Lord" (Dies Domini) to remind us of these things. It's time for us to reclaim Sunday. One way to do this is by taking care of errands on Saturday instead of Sunday. Another way is to be creative in planning activities together and establishing family traditions. You might, for instance, reserve a certain tablecloth for Sunday use only, special table mats, certain toys or games—even a favorite meal. Here are some activities your family might engage in to make Sunday special:

- Talk to one another.
- Play a board game.
- Go for a ride.
- Visit friends and relatives.
- Invite someone to a meal.
- Hold a family meeting or a family night.
- Enjoy a cultural activity.
- Have a picnic.
- Ride bicycles or go rollerblading.
- Participate in an activity to help the needy.
- Do something kind for a neighbor.
- Throw a party.
- Spend time with an elderly person who might be lonesome.
- Prepare a meal together.
- Hold a special prayer service.
- Participate in a sports activity.
- Make cookies.
- Visit someone who is sick.

Celebrating Fridays

Before the reforms of Vatican II, Catholics did not eat meat on Fridays. Although this law was abolished, our bishops stated that we should still perform some penance on Fridays. We are responsible for observing Friday as the day of Our Lord's passion and death. As a family, you might decide on some sacrifice or good work that you will do together on Fridays such as skipping dessert or helping out in a soup kitchen.

Celebrating Kwanzaa

Kwanzaa is a seven-day celebration from December 26 to New Year's Day during which the black community celebrates black culture. It commemorates the importance of the community and the family. The word Kwanzaa is Swahili for "first fruits of the harvest." From its origin in 1966, Kwanzaa has promoted pride in the black community and has heightened awareness of the African-American culture. Each day focuses on one principle that black Americans strive to live by:

December 26	Unity (Umoja)
December 27	Self-determination (Kujichagulia)
December 28	Collective work and responsibility (Ujima)
December 29	Cooperative economics (Ujamaa)
December 30	Purpose (Nia)
December 31	Creativity (Kuumba)
January 1	Faith (Imani)

To join in Kwanzaa your family might discuss the respective principle each day. You also might set up a Kwanzaa table. Cover it with a colorful straw mat symbolizing the past and tradition. On the table set the following objects:

- A seven-branched candleholder that stands for the principles. The center candle is black. Three red candles are on one side, and three green candles are on the other. On the first day, the black candle is lit; on the second day the black candle and one red candle are lit; on the third day a green candle is also lit. Continue each day alternating between red and green. Black stands for the color of the African people, red for their suffering, and green for hope and the lush foliage of Africa.
- A communal cup to represent sharing
- Fruits and vegetables representing the results of people working together. There is an ear of corn for each child.
- Small, homemade gifts.

Celebrating New Year's Day

New Year's Eve is a good time for holding a reconciliation prayer service. New Year's Day marks a fresh start on life. Make resolutions to improve the way you live. Have family members write these on slips of paper. If you wish, share the resolutions and be accountable to each other for them. At a special meal thank God for the favors of the past year. Then ask God to bless your new year. As part of the prayer, let each family member state a wish for the year. For dessert serve fortune cookies.

Fortune Cookies Write fitting resolutions or Scripture verses on slips of paper. Then follow this recipe:

4 egg whites	1/4 teaspoon salt
1 cup sugar	1/2 teaspoon vanilla
1/2 cup butter	2 tablespoons water
1/2 cup sifted flour	

Add sugar to egg whites and blend until fluffy. Melt the butter and let it cool slightly. Add flour, salt, vanilla, water, and butter to mixture. Beat until smooth. Pour batter from a spoon in 3-inch circles onto a well-greased cookie sheet. Bake at 375° for 8 minutes. While the cookies are warm, put a slip of paper on each circle, fold the cookie in half and bend it in the middle to curve. If the cookies get too hard to work with, put them back in the oven for a minute.

Days to Celebrate

Here are some other days that lend themselves to celebrating in the family. You can find others on a Catholic calendar. Include prayer and special food as part of your celebration.

New Year's Day
Martin Luther King, Jr. Day
Arbor Day
Groundhog Day
Valentine's Day
Presidents' Day
St. Patrick's Day
First day of Spring
April Fool's Day

Earth Day
Mother's Day
Memorial Day
Flag Day
Epiphany
Grandparents Day
Annunciation of the Lord
Father's Day
All Saints Day
All Souls Day
Ash Wednesday
Pentecost
Solemnity of the Body and Blood of Christ
Feasts of Mary (Assumption, Birthday, Immaculate Conception, etc.)
Ascension
Labor Day
Solemnity of Christ the King
Veterans Day
Thanksgiving Day
Feast of the Holy Family
A favorite saint's feast day

Family Albums and Videos

Keep family photo albums or make videos of family celebrations in order to strengthen family identity and to preserve memories. Include the family members' celebrations of the sacraments.

FOR REFLECTION

- What rituals does your family practice? What new ones would you like to adopt?

- What holyday or holiday could you make special by a family celebration? How?

- Would your family benefit from having a ritual to reconcile when someone has hurt the others and needs to forgive and be forgiven?

- How can your family make Sunday more special?

5

Family Projects

The French author Anatole France related that as a child he read about St. Simeon Stylites who, in the fifth century, lived atop a pillar as penance. The boy Anatole attempted to imitate this ascetic by placing a chair on the kitchen table and sitting on it. When it was time for dinner, his mother ordered him to climb down and remove the chair. Anatole wrote, "I concluded that it is difficult to become a saint in a family." Yet, this should be one of the chief goals of Catholic families, that is, to raise saints.

We become saints through our interactions with those with whom we live. Our relationships with them, how well we have loved them, determine our eternal destiny. To love these people God chose for our lives, we must know them. To know them, we must spend time together. Following are a few ways for family members to enjoy one another's company and at the same time, build faith.

Ideas for Family Projects

One example of a project that promotes family unity is a Booster Box. The family decorates a shoebox together. Then each person writes something positive about every other family member on slips of paper and puts them in the box. On a special occasion or at an ordinary family meal these slips are read aloud. The box can also be used for boosting family members' self-esteem on their birthdays. In this case, everyone writes something special about the birthday person. Other possible family projects are these:

• Celebrating namedays or feast days

• Choosing a family patron saint

• Creating a family coat of arms

• Telling the stories of your patron saints

- Making a Mary mobile
- Adopting a missionary
- Gathering materials to be recycled
- Writing a family creed
- Setting up a prayer corner at home
- Watching a TV program or video together then talking about it
- Visiting different churches or shrines
- Making a family Advent wreath
- Making a Jesse tree
- Composing a family prayer
- Writing a family creed or mission statement
- Working on a Habitat for Humanity house
- Making a family candle that is used for special occasions
- Celebrating the sacrament of reconciliation as a family
- Participating in a marathon for a worthy cause
- Putting together a family album
- Volunteering at a soup kitchen
- Preparing a Sunday liturgy together
- Planting or adopting a tree
- Making a quilt of ways God has blessed the family
- Choosing a family motto
- Adopting another family (visiting them, bringing them a meal, giving them tickets to events)
- Beautifying one corner of the world

Can you think of other projects to unite and strengthen your family life?

Plugging into Neighborhood Offerings

Be attuned to events in your diocese and parish that you could participate in as a family: a lecture, workshop, mission, or retreat day. For

instance, in Cleveland, Ohio, there is an annual march protesting violence against women. The march is sponsored by the Ursuline Sisters
who have suffered the murder of two members. By joining in this pub-
lic event, a family would practice faith in action.

Be informed about cultural activities in town that tie in with faith.
For example, sixth-graders who are studying the Old Testament would
no doubt enjoy seeing the play *Joseph and the Amazing Technicolor
Dreamcoat* with their families.

Recently programs on Mary, the apostles, St. Patrick, as well as two
specials on the life of Jesus have been broadcast. Look for television
programs on religious topics like these and watch and discuss them
together. You might be able to tune in to the Odyssey interfaith cable
network or the Eternal Word Television Network (EWTN), which both
provide religious programs. When a good show is on past your children's bedtime, tape it for viewing later.

Television can also be an effective way to instill Christian values in
the children. After viewing a show together, discuss the morality of the
characters' actions. Point out what was in line with Jesus' teaching and
what wasn't.

Visit an art museum and focus on religious works. A guide might be
happy to help you plan your tour. Use masterpieces as a springboard
for faith education as well as faith sharing.

Parks and vacation spots are a natural way to introduce your children to the good, powerful God who created our beautiful planet.
What better way to teach about God's wisdom and love than by point-
ing out the lavish and intricate gifts of creation? Walking outside with
your children, enjoying the wonders of nature, is conducive to conver-
sation on a deeper level.

Hospitality

One way to live as Christ taught is to offer hospitality, not only to
friends and to those who have invited you to their home, but to
strangers and those in need. In these days when too often neighbors
scarcely know one another, much less share lives, this practice is strik-
ingly countercultural! It takes courage to open your door to anyone
with the words, "My house is your house" on your lips. One family I

know decided to share their family life with others. Over the course of two years they opened their home in Florida to more than fifty guests: friends in trouble, people who came to the rectory for help, foster children, even a family from Canada whose son had broken his neck while on a golf tour. Your family might imitate them to some extent. In the process, your own family life will be enriched.

Finding Other Ideas

Adopt family activities that you hear about or discover in reading. Here are two examples:

Family Pledge of Nonviolence

Making peace must start within ourselves and in our family. Each of us, members of the (*name*) family, commits ourselves as best we can to become nonviolent and peaceable people.

To Respect Self and Others

I promise to respect myself, to affirm others and to avoid uncaring criticism, hateful words, physical attacks, and self-destructive behavior.

To Communicate Better

I promise to share my feelings honestly, to look for safe ways to express my anger, and to work at solving problems peacefully.

To Listen

I promise to listen carefully to others, especially those who disagree with me, and to consider others' feelings and needs rather than insist on having my own way.

To Forgive

I promise to apologize and make amends when I have hurt someone, to forgive others, and to keep from holding grudges.

To Respect Nature

I promise to treat the environment and all living things, including our pets, with respect and care.

To Play Creatively

I promise to select entertainment and toys that support our family's values and to avoid entertainment that makes violence look exciting, funny, or acceptable.

To Be Courageous
I promise to challenge violence in all its forms whenever I encounter it, whether at home, at school, at work, or in the community, and to stand up with others who are treated unfairly.

This is our pledge. These are our goals. We will check ourselves on what we have pledged once a month on (day/date) for the next twelve months so that we can help each other become a more peaceable family.

All pray together…
Loving God, you sent Jesus to show us how to live nonviolently. Jesus, you listened carefully to everyone. You cared about the feelings of others. You forgave those who hurt you. Your heart went out to people no one else cared about. Jesus, send us your Spirit to help each of us be truthful whenever we speak, loving whenever we act, and courageous whenever we find violence or injustice around us. We make our Family Pledge counting on your mercy and love to help us live it faithfully.

Unleavened Bread for First Communion
This is a very simple recipe to do with your child. You might want to make this bread the night before First Communion. You can then share the bread at a meal the next day, or use it in a family prayer service to celebrate the event.

1/2 cup (one stick) margarine, melted
1 cup water
1/2 cup honey
2 cups white flour
1 1/2 cups wheat flour
1/2 tsp. salt
1/2 tsp. baking soda
1/2 tsp. baking powder

Combine the first three ingredients in a bowl. Combine all the dry ingredients in a larger bowl; mix thoroughly. Add liquid ingredients to the dry, and blend. Knead lightly. Roll out on a floured board and cut or shape to desired size. The dough should be *flat*, not shaped like a loaf. It may be scored for easy breaking. Use a glass to press in the center circle, and use a butter knife to score the other lines.

Bake on an ungreased cookie sheet at 375° for 10 to 15 minutes. (Time will depend on the thickness of your dough; edges will be brown when the bread is done.)

FOR REFLECTION

- When is the last time you did something together as a family?

- What family project mentioned in this chapter appeals to you as one you might like to try with your family?

- What programs for helping the needy might you participate in as a family?

- What television program scheduled this week would be a good springboard for family discussion?

- How can you practice the virtue of hospitality to a greater extent?

6

Advent Activities

Advent activities in the home can help immunize the children against the hectic pace and commercialism that tend to characterize these weeks before Christmas. Family religious rites and prayers can keep everyone focused on the coming of the Savior. You may wish to try some of the following traditional Advent practices.

Advent Wreath Set four candles on a circle of evergreens: three purple and one pink. (Or use white candles and colored bows.) The circle stands for God's unending love, and the evergreen stands for hope and life. The four candles represent the four weeks of Advent as well as the many years the human race waited for the Savior.

On the evening before each Sunday in Advent, light a candle. The pink candle is lighted on the third Sunday because pink stands for joy and we are happy that Christmas is almost here. When you light the candle, pray an Advent wreath prayer. You might also sing an Advent song. Compose your own prayers or use prayers from a missalette or those that follow.

• First Sunday

Leader: Jesus, in our darkness be our light. Show us the way to truth and life. Let us reflect you to others.

All respond: Come, Lord Jesus!

• Second Sunday

Leader: Jesus, in our coldness be our warmth. Give us comfort and hope in the trials and hardships of life. Thaw our hearts with divine love that reaches out to others.

All respond: Come, Lord Jesus!

• Third Sunday

Leader: Jesus, in our sadness and anxiety be our joy. Overcome our fear of death, sin, and evil with the power of your love. Let our rejoicing brighten the lives of others.

All respond: Come, Lord Jesus!

• Fourth Sunday

Leader: Jesus, be Emmanuel, God with us. Strengthen us with your grace to live the way you taught. Bring us all to the kingdom you won for us by becoming one of us.

All respond: Come, Lord Jesus!

The Jesse Tree—The Family Tree of Jesus Jesse is King David's father, an ancestor of Jesus. The Jesse Tree is decorated with symbols of people and events related to Jesus' coming. Use an artificial tree, a real tree limb, a tree made on a large piece of felt or paper, or your Christmas tree.

Symbols
Apple with two bites out of it (Adam, Eve)
Ark or rainbow (Noah)
Bundle of twigs, ram in bush (Abraham, Isaac)
Pitcher (Rebecca)
Ladder (Jacob)
Well or coat of many colors (Joseph)
Burning bush or tablets of the Law (Moses)
Sword (Judith)
Sheaf of wheat (Ruth)
Shepherd's staff or root, stem, and flower (Jesse)
Harp, key, or crown and scepter (David)
Temple or scale of justice (Solomon)
Whale (Jonah)
Scroll (Isaiah)
Six-pointed star and chain (Esther)
Baptismal shell (John the Baptist)
Carpentry tools: hammer, saw, chisel, angle, and plane (Joseph)
Lily, crown circled by stars or decorative M (Mary)
Bethlehem, rising sun (Jesus)
Chi-rho for treetop (Jesus)

Straw for the Crib Set a box or empty crib where it is easily seen. Each night the children (and parents too) place a piece of straw in the crib (or yellow yarn or paper strip) for every kind act done that day. On Christmas Eve, when the crib is filled with straw, the figure of the Infant Jesus is placed in it.

Kristkindl The word "Kristkindl" is German for "Christ Child." Family members draw names for a Kristkindl (also called a "Kris Kringle"), a person for whom they will secretly pray and do favors during Advent. In this way, they prepare for Jesus by showing love.

The Christ Candle Decorate a large candle with symbols of Christ such as the chi-rho. Carve the designs, draw them with felt-tipped pens, or press beads or sequins into the candle wax. Add a ribbon. Place the candle in a holder and cover it with blue silk, net, or lace as a symbol of Our Lady's mantle. On Christmas Eve remove the mantle and light the candle. Also, light it at dinner on the twelve days after Christmas. The flame stands for Christ, the Light of the World.

Road to Bethlehem Make a road of twenty-four stones leading to a scene of Bethlehem. Let the children color a stone each day of Advent.

A Waiting Chain Have the children make a chain with twenty-four links made out of loops of construction paper. Loops can contain Scripture verses or good deeds for the day. Paste one end of the chain to a nativity picture from a Christmas card. Each day during Advent clip a loop off.

Christmas Cards Send Christmas cards that have a religious theme so that the real meaning of Christmas is reinforced for your children as well as for your relatives and friends. Every night, as a family, go through the cards that arrived that day. Read the greeting on each one and pray for the person who sent it. (Or after Christmas you might remove one card each day, read it, and pray for the sender.)

Gifts for Others Give money, gifts, or time to a group or organization that helps the poor. Buy Christmas gifts from organizations that support the needy.

Homemade Gifts Have each member of the family make gifts for the others. These may be gift certificates with promises to do services, such as washing dishes or polishing shoes.

Surprise Envelopes For each day of Advent prepare an envelope with a way to celebrate enclosed. Work together to plan the contents: a poem, prayer, picture, or activity: "Everyone will help with supper." "The one who opens this will make an ornament for the tree." "Someone will do dishes for the one who opens this." "All will pray silently for five minutes now." Every day during Advent let someone open an envelope.

Home Decorations Here are three ideas: 1.) Make an Advent banner or poster with a caption like "Come, Lord Jesus." On the other side, design a Christmas banner. 2.) Arrange a table centerpiece that changes each week. 3.) Construct a mobile using Christmas pictures and Advent Scripture verses on various shaped colored paper. Use yarn or string to hang the paper from a hanger.

Advent Calendar Make an Advent calendar to help count down the days before Christmas. In each block write a good deed or Advent practice that family members will try to do on the respective day. (If you don't want to make your own, assorted types of Advent calendars can be found in religious goods stores.)

Advent House To mark the days from December 17 until Christmas Eve, make an Advent house. Cover a shoebox with paper. Draw a symbol for each of the O antiphons (see next page) on paper and paste them on the side of the box. From construction paper cut out seven squares large enough to cover the antiphons. Decorate the squares to look like windows and write the antiphon's date on it. Put a window over each antiphon, using a single small piece of tape for each. Inside the box put a picture of the nativity, cut from a Christmas card. Beginning with December 17, remove a window each day and pray the matching antiphon. On the evening of December 24 remove the picture of the nativity and stand it on the box.

O Antiphon Cookies

Make sugar cookies in the shape of symbols for the O antiphons. Cut out the patterns from paper.

Symbols

December 17: oil lamp

December 18: tablets of law

December 19: flower

December 20: key

December 21: sun

December 22: crown

December 23: manger

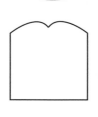

O Antiphons

The O antiphons are the Alleluia verses of the Masses for the last seven days before Christmas. Each one of them is a verse of the song "O Come, O Come Emmanuel." Each begins with a different way of addressing Christ. Your family might pray the antiphon of the day around the Advent wreath.

December 17

O Wisdom, who issued from the mouth of the Most High,
    reaching from beginning to end,
    ordering all things mightily and tenderly,
Come to teach us the way of prudence.

December 18

O Lord of Lords and Leader of the house of Israel,
    Who appeared to Moses in the bush's flaming fire,
    and gave to him the Law of Sinai—
Come to redeem us with outstretched arms.

December 19

O root of Jesse, a standard to the people,

before whom kings are silent,
to whom all nations shall appeal—
Come to deliver us; delay, please, no longer.

December 20
O *key of David*, and scepter of the house of Israel,
You open and no one dares shut,
You shut and no one dares open—
Come, deliver from the chains of prison him who sits
in darkness and in the shadow of death.

December 21
O *rising dawn*, radiance of eternal light
and sun of justice—
Come, enlighten those sitting in darkness and in the shadow
of death.

December 22
O *king of nations*, and their desired one,
cornerstone who binds two into one—
Come and save us whom you fashioned from the dust
of the earth.

December 23
O *Emmanuel*, God-with-us, our King and Lawgiver,
the awaited of the peoples and their Savior—
Come to save us, O Lord, our God.

FOR REFLECTION

- What spirit and qualities would you like to see develop in your children during Advent?

- Which suggested customs would be appropriate for your family to try this year?

- What activity can you eliminate from your life in order to make Advent less hectic?

7

Christmas Activities

In her book *Gold in Your Memories* (Ave Maria Press, 1998) Sister Macrina Wiederkehr tells how, in her family, on Christmas Eve the children gathered in the kitchen where they enjoyed popcorn or some other treat while Santa was putting out gifts in the next room. Then their mother said, "Let's turn out the lights and sit here and wait in the darkness." They "waited for Jesus" until the light in the next room went out. Then everyone was given a sparkler, and all walked silently into the next room. The sparklers were lit, and the tree lights were turned on. Like Sister Macrina, we all have our own precious memories of Christmas.

Christmas is the ultimate family feast. Not only does it mark the birth of the first Christian family, but the rituals that surround the celebration of Christmas have power to promote love and unity among family members. In the course of time, each nationality has produced its own rich collection of Christmas customs. These are worth exploring. Make your family Christmases more memorable and faith-filled by adopting them or some of the following ideas.

Christmas Customs

Journey to Bethlehem During the last week of Advent, reenact the journey of Mary and Joseph. Take their figures from the nativity set to the farthest room in the house. Process and sing carols each day as you carry the figures closer to the crib scene. On Christmas Eve process with lit candles and let the youngest child set the figures in place. Later that night you can place the baby Jesus in the crib.

Homemade Ornaments   Make a special ornament for the family Christmas tree each year.

A Chrismon Tree A chrismon originally was a monogram of Christ, specifically the chi-rho (see p. 38). Today it refers to a Christmas tree ornament based on a Christian symbol. Chrismons are usually made

42

with gold and white materials. Add some chrismons to your Christmas decorations to recall the true meaning of Christmas.

Symbols

• Chi-rho: an X with a P superimposed; the first two letters of the Greek word *christos,* which means Christ

• Circle: Christ the eternal one

• IHS: first three letters of the Greek word for Jesus

• Crown: Christ, king of the universe

• Fish: symbol for Christ; the initials of the words "Christ, Son of God, Savior" spell fish in Greek; the letters IXOYC may be written inside

• Shepherd's staff: the Good Shepherd

• Anchor with cross

• Sun

• Sphere with cross on top

• Cross

• Five-pointed star with a rose inside: rose stands for human nature; star for divinity

• Three entwined circles: the Trinity

• Triangle and trefoil combined: symbol of the Triune God

• Cross inside a diamond: spread of the Gospel to the four corners of the earth

• Chi-rho with alpha and omega

• Greek cross: arms of equal length

• Greek cross superimposed over sun with one letter of the word NIKA in each quadrant (NIKA is Greek for "conquer").

Original Nativity Scene Let each member of the family make a figure in the nativity set. Use clay, dough, or other creative materials.

Candle in the Window Put a candle in your window as a symbol that you wish to welcome the Holy Family.

Christmas Tree Blessing Before lighting the tree, bless it. Reflect on the role a tree played in the first sin and the tree on which Jesus saved us. Pray that the light of Christ may shine forth from each family member.

Manger Scene Blessing On Christmas Eve bless your manger scene.

Christmas Carols Sing or play Christmas carols or attend a concert of Christmas carols so that your children are as familiar with religious songs as they are with "Jingle Bells" and "Santa Claus Is Coming to Town."

Christmas Eve Gather around the crib scene and read aloud the story of the first Christmas from Luke 2:1–21. Sing "Silent Night." Make it a tradition to have special food that night.

Birthday Cake Make a birthday cake for Jesus. Let everyone help decorate it.

Gift to Jesus Pass out slips of paper and have the family members write down a gift each will give Jesus. They might simply write their name. Put the slips in a box. Gift wrap the box, mark it with a tag "To Jesus," and set it under the tree.

Posada The posada is a Hispanic tradition. *Posada* means "inn" or "shelter." At dusk, people go door to door, replaying Mary and Joseph's search for a place to stay in Bethlehem. Two children carry a tray holding statues of Mary and Joseph encircled by evergreens. The group sings about the first Christmas. At each house, the children knock and ask for shelter. Those inside reply that there is no room. Finally at one house the children are told, "Enter, holy pilgrims. This night is one of joy, for we shelter the Mother of God." Everyone enters and kneels in prayer, asking that the Christ Child may enter their homes and hearts. Then refreshments are served. The children take turns being blindfolded and swing, with a stick, at a piñata filled with candy and prizes. When the piñata is broken open, its treasures are shared by all. Organize a posada for your neighborhood, or hold one in your own home by processing around your house knocking on different doors.

Oplatki Adopt the Polish custom of oplatki at Christmas. This is a wafer of bread, similar to a Communion host, that is stamped with a nativity scene. On Christmas Eve two circles of oplatki are notched from one edge to the center and slid into each other to form a globe, which is then suspended over the dinner table. The family begins the meal by blessing a large piece of oplatki, and then breaking and sharing it with everyone gathered.

Hiding Baby Jesus Hide the statue of the Baby Jesus on Christmas Eve. Have the children find the statue and place it in the manger.

Christmas Stories Read Christmas stories such as the following:

The Story of the Candy Cane
It is said that a candymaker in Indiana created what we know today as the Christmas candy cane. Originally intending it to be a witness to the faith, he made it a symbol of Christ's life. He decided to make it hard candy to stand for Jesus as the rock, the foundation of the church. He began with a stick of pure white to symbolize the sinlessness of Jesus and his Virgin Birth. The shape he chose was a cane because it looks like the staff of the Good Shepherd, who lovingly seeks after the sinners that stray from the fold. In addition, if you turn the cane upside-down, it forms the letter "J" for Jesus, the Savior.

The candymaker decorated the white stick with red stripes. One large red stripe was for the blood Jesus shed on the cross for us. Three smaller stripes stood for the stripes of the scourging Jesus underwent for us and by which he saved us.

Whether or not the story is true, a candy cane can remind us of the wonder of Jesus who made our lives sweet again by the gift of eternal life.

• Decorate your Christmas tree with candy canes.

• Let the children help you bake candy cane cookies for Christmas.

Twelve Days of Christmas To extend the celebration of Christmas throughout the Christmas season, let each person open a small gift every day until Epiphany. A variation of this is to spread the opening of Christmas gifts over these days. An added benefit of this practice is that, because they are not overwhelmed with a pile of presents, the children will better appreciate each gift.

Epiphany Customs

"On entering the house, they (the Magi) saw the child with Mary his mother; and they knelt down and paid him homage" (Matthew 2:11). The Feast of Epiphany, also called Little Christmas and Twelfth Night, is one of the oldest feasts of Christianity. It commemorates the Magi's visit to the child Jesus, when the Good News of the savior's birth was revealed to Gentiles. Several traditions have arisen in celebration of this feast. Here are some ways to observe Epiphany:

The Progress of the Magi Set the statues of the three kings riding on their camels some distance away from the nativity scene. Every day move them a little closer until on Epiphany they are around the crib.

Home Blessing The leader accompanied by the family goes from room to room blessing the house with holy water and praying a prayer such as the following: "Lord, our God, bless this home that it may be holy and full of life. May it be a place of laughter, work and prayer, peace and love. Keep in your care all who live and enter here. This we ask, Father, Son, and Holy Spirit. Amen." Or simply: "We bless this room in thanksgiving to God the Father, Son, and Holy Spirit. Amen."

The leader marks one of the doorways with colored chalk, writing the two halves of the year on either side of the initials of the three Magi (Caspar, Melchior, and Balthazar):

$$20 + C + M + B + 01$$

Three Kings' Cake Epiphany is celebrated in Europe with a Three Kings' Cake. Inside the cake, which is like a large cookie, there is a dried bean, a thimble, a dime, or another treasure. Whoever finds the object in his or her piece of cake supposedly will have wealth in the coming year or become king or queen of an Epiphany party. To avoid having someone break a tooth, you might simply make a cake in shape of a crown, such as a bundt cake or angel food cake, with gumdrop or jellybean jewels. Or, you can make crown-shaped cookies.

Mission Activities Hold a prayer service for the missions that incorporates the song "We Three Kings." Decide on a family project to raise funds to send to the missions.

FOR REFLECTION

• What Christmas customs do you remember from your childhood?

• Which customs in this chapter are most practical and possible for your family to carry out?

• How can your family pay more attention to the feast of the Epiphany?

8

Lenten Activities

Lent is the springtime of the liturgical year, a time of growth and change. We prepare again to celebrate the great paschal mystery of Christ by making ourselves more worthy of his love and forgiveness. During the forty days of Lent, use some of the following activities to create a new heart in your family members.

Mardi Gras Long ago in Western Europe because the use of meat and fats was limited during Lent and refrigerating fresh food was difficult, people used up what they had on hand by making special food. On the Tuesday before Ash Wednesday they would eat fat cakes, or what we call pancakes. They would also hold a carnival (from the Latin *carne vale* which means "farewell to meat"). The day before Lent became known as Mardi Gras, French for "Fat Tuesday."

For breakfast or supper have extra rich pancakes served with syrup, warmed applesauce, strawberries, cherries, or fruit preserves. Have a party the night before Lent begins.

Ash Wednesday Burn the palm from the previous year. Use the ashes to make a sign of the cross on the children's foreheads. Bury the ashes outside.

Burying the Alleluia Alleluia, which means "Praise the Lord," is a word of rejoicing. During the somber season of Lent, we do not say it. Keep a small flag that says "alleluia" at your family prayer corner. On Ash Wednesday put the flag (or a paper with "alleluia" written on it) in a box covered with purple paper and marked with a silver cross. Hide the box until Easter.

Parish Activities As a family attend parish lenten activities such as the Stations of the Cross, a simple supper for Operation Rice Bowl, a performance of the Passion, or a lenten lecture series.

Clay Pot Shatter an inexpensive clay pot and give each family member a piece to keep during Lent as a reminder that we are like clay in God's hands. During Lent, we can allow God to shape us into new vessels.

Planting Seeds Plant seeds and watch them burst forth with new life during Lent. Have each family member fill half of an eggshell with soil and plant a few marigold, petunia, or grass seeds in it.

Tree of Life Put some branches loosely in a can or set them in plaster of Paris. Make caterpillars out of pipecleaners and butterflies out of paper. Fasten the caterpillars to the branches. Each time a family member does a good deed, he or she may replace a caterpillar with a butterfly. By Easter, the tree should be full of colorful butterflies.

Pretzels During Lent serve pretzels that are in the shape of arms crossed in prayer. The name "pretzel" comes from *bracellae*, the Latin word for "arms."

Recipe for Pretzels

1 package of yeast	4 1/2 cups flour
1 1/2 cups warm water	2 tablespoons water
1 egg yolk	coarse salt
1/2 teaspoon sugar	

Dissolve yeast in the water and add sugar. Stir in flour and knead for six minutes. Cover dough in a greased bowl and let it rise until double in size. Divide the dough into 14 pieces and roll out into bread sticks. Whip the egg yolk and two tablespoons of water together and brush lightly over the sticks. Sprinkle the salt over them and bend them into a pretzel shape with the two arms crossed and resting at the top of the loop. Bake for 12 minutes at 450° on a non-stick cookie sheet.

Hot Cross Buns Serve hot cross buns especially on Ash Wednesday and Good Friday. These are made from sweet dough laced with citron and raisins. They have a white frosting cross on top. You might purchase cinnamon rolls and make them into hot cross buns.

Mosaic Cross Cut out a large cardboard cross and many squares of colored paper. During Lent whenever a family member does a good deed or makes a sacrifice, he or she glues a square to the cross. Your aim could be to cover the cross before Easter.

Passion Sunday Have a procession at home with palms, songs, and instruments. Braid the palm or make simple crosses out of it. Display the finished products.

Spring Flowers At the end of September plant the bulbs of crocus, tulips, daffodils, or hyacinths, placing them to form a cross, an egg, a banner, or a word or phrase such as *Alleluia, new life,* or *He is risen.* Hold a prayer celebration by sprinkling the bulbs in the ground with holy water and reading Jesus' words in John 12:24. In the spring the flowers will declare an Easter message. If you prefer a more reliable alternative for Easter Day, "plant" colorful Easter eggs in the ground in the shape of an Easter symbol.

Alms Box Decorate a box and put a slit in the top. During Lent put money in the box that family members save by fasting (for example from dessert) or by sacrificing (for example, not going to a movie). Donate the money to a worthy cause, such as the Easter Seal Society, which assists children who have disabilities.

Family Penances In addition to observing the laws of fasting and abstinence, perform a lenten penance together. To promote self-control give up candy, gum, soft drinks, dessert, or snacks between meals. Limit the watching of TV or videos or listening to music. Choose a penance that benefits needy persons, such as spending time with them or doing something difficult for them.

Spring Cleaning As a family, renew a corner of your home: the attic, the garage, or the yard. Paint a room or clean out closets. Give unused toys and clothes to the poor. Hold a garage sale and donate the profits to a charitable organization.

A Passion Tree or Passion Eggs Set branches in plaster of Paris and decorate them with miniature objects related to Our Lord's Passion and death: towel, host and chalice, bag of thirty pieces of silver, rooster, whip, red cloak, crown of thorns, Veronica's veil, cross, nails, INRI sign, vinegar, heart, spear, dice, clock showing 3:00 PM. Instead of making a tree, you can obtain plastic Easter eggs that can be opened. Place the items inside the eggs. At appropriate times during Lent and the Triduum, open an egg and talk about the item inside.

FOR REFLECTION

- Which activities would make Lent more meaningful for your family?

- What lenten programs are available in your parish for you to join as a family?

- Prayer, fasting, and almsgiving are the three actions of Lent. Think about then discuss some of the ways your family can practice each of these actions during Lent.

9

Easter Activities

Our whole faith depends on the Lord's resurrection. Because Jesus lives, we know that his words were true and that we too can live forever. Every Sunday we celebrate the Lord's death and resurrection, and for this reason Sunday is called a little Easter. But once a year we celebrate the paschal mystery in grand style during the Easter season. Intensify your family celebration of Easter, the greatest and holiest feast of the year, by adopting some of these ideas:

Easter Triduum Join in your parish celebration of these three holy days. If possible, attend the diocesan Chrism Mass. Be present, especially, for the dramatic Easter Vigil services when new members are incorporated into the church. Enhance your observance of these days at home in the following ways:

Holy Thursday Hold or participate in a Seder meal (Passover meal) with a Christian theme. There is a model for a seder meal in *Leading Students Into Scripture* by Kathleen Glavich, SND. For more complete information see *Celebrating an Authentic Passover Seder* by Joseph M. Stallings, published by Resource Publications, Inc.

Good Friday Make the dining room bare with only a simple cross on the table. Be quiet: no TV, radio, CD player, or computer. Try not to talk from 12:00 until 3:00 PM. Serve simple meals.

Holy Saturday Participate in the blessing of Easter foods at your parish or hold your own blessing ceremony. Take home some water blessed at the Easter Vigil. Use it for blessings.

Luminaria Make a little lantern. Turn down the top of a small paper bag to make a firm rim. Cut little crosses or other symbols out of the bag so that the light will shine through it. (Don't make the designs too big, or the wind might blow out the candle.) Then fill the bag one-fourth full of sand, dirt, or kitty litter. Place a small candle in the center of the sand and anchor it so that it stands upright. Set the bag in your front yard or set several luminaria along the walk of your front yard. Light the candles at sundown. They will go out when they reach the level of the sand. (Instead of paper bags, you can use plastic milk cartons.)

Easter Candle Make a family Easter candle. Use contact paper, red fingernail polish, paint, or permanent markers to make a large plus sign (cross) on the candle. Put a numeral of the current year in each quadrant, going across. Make an alpha above this plus sign and an omega below it. Set five red tacks, pins, cloves, or grains of incense in the candle at the four ends of the cross and the center. Light the candle on Easter and during the Easter season. Each time you light it pray "Light of Christ," to which all respond "Thanks be to God."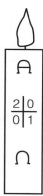

Easter Sunrise Wake up in time to watch the sunrise. Have a sunrise picnic breakfast. Read the Easter story from the Bible (Mark 16:1–8). Sing or play a rousing Easter song, such as the "Hallelujah" chorus from Handel's *Messiah.*

Easter Walk On Easter go on a new-life walk together, noticing signs of new life.

Lamb Cake Make a "lamb cake" using coconut for wool, a raisin for an eye, and a cherry mouth. The lamb is a symbol of Jesus, the paschal lamb who was sacrificed for us.

Cross Cake Make a "cross cake" by baking two cakes in oblong pans. Cut one cake in thirds and place a third at the top and two sides of the other cake to form a cross. Then frost the cake.

Easter Bunny Salad Because rabbits are so prolific they are a symbol of the abundant life Easter brings. Make salad in the form of a rabbit head. For each serving, set half of a pear as the head on a lettuce leaf. Decorate the head using carrot or celery sticks for ears; raisins, olives, or grape halves for eyes; and a cherry for a mouth. For whiskers, use spaghetti sticks or string licorice, or draw them in with cream cheese.

Easter Bread Make Easter bread, a symbol of new life. Try recipes from various nationalities. One kind of Easter bread has whole eggs in their shells set in the dough; another has braided dough along the perimeter to resemble the crown of thorns.

Eggs A chick emerging from an egg represents Christ coming out of the tomb. Decorate Easter eggs. Try different methods, perhaps using Ukrainian symbols. Bless the eggs. Make Easter baskets and give them to friends and neighbors. Make one basket your centerpiece. Hang some decorated eggs on a tree outside.

Egg Hunt On Easter have an egg hunt. Mark one egg as a special egg. Award a prize to the one who finds the most eggs. Let the person who finds the special egg use it to tap everyone else's eggs open, so that the eggs can be eaten.

New Clothes New clothes on Easter stand for the new life we have through Christ's death and resurrection. We wear them as a sign that we have "put on Christ." Plan to have everyone wear at least one new article of clothing on Easter.

Butterflies Make butterflies, which are a favorite symbol of transformation, out of cloth or paper and decorate your home with them. Give everyone a butterfly card, pin, or bookmark as an Easter memento.

Banner Make a family Easter banner out of paper, felt, or burlap.

Resurrection Day Story Cookies
To be made the evening before Easter.

Ingredients	*Supplies*
1 cup whole pecans	zipper baggie
1 tsp. vinegar	wooden spoon
3 egg whites	mixing bowl
pinch of salt	cookie sheet
1 cup sugar	wax paper
	tape
	Bible

Preheat oven to 300°.

Place pecans in zipper baggie and let children beat them into pieces

with the wooden spoon.
- Explain that after Jesus was arrested the Roman soldiers beat him.
  Read John 19:1–3 to the children.

Let each child smell the vinegar. Put 1 tsp. vinegar into the mixing bowl.
- Explain that when Jesus was thirsty on the cross he was given vinegar to drink.
  Read John 19:28–30.

Add egg whites to vinegar.
- Explain that eggs represent life. Jesus gave his life to give us life.
  Read John 10:10–11.

Sprinkle a little salt into each child's hand. Let them taste it and brush the rest into the bowl.
- Explain that this represents the salty tears shed by Jesus' followers and the bitterness of our own sin.
  Read Luke 23:27.

Comment that so far the ingredients are not very appetizing.
Add 1 cup sugar.
- Explain that the sweetest part of the story is that Jesus died because he loves us. He wants us to know and belong to him.
  Read Psalm 34:8 and John 3:16.

Beat with a mixer on high speed until stiff peaks are formed. This can take quite some time, so you might want to sing a song or two together while you wait.
- Explain that the color white represents the purity in God's eyes of those whose sins have been cleansed by Jesus.
  Read Isaiah 1:18 and John 3:1–3.

Fold in broken nuts.
Drop by teaspoons onto cookie sheet covered by wax paper.
- Explain that each mound represents the rocky tomb where Jesus'

body was laid.
   Read Matthew 27:57–60.

Put the cookie sheet in the oven, close the door and turn the oven OFF. Give each child a piece of tape and seal the oven door.
* Explain that Jesus' tomb was sealed.
   Read Matthew 27:65–66.

Tell the children to go to bed!
* Explain that they may feel sad to leave the cookies in the oven overnight. Jesus' followers were in despair when the tomb was sealed.
   Read John 16:20, 22.

On Easter morning, open the oven and give everyone a cookie. Notice the cracked surface and take a bite. The cookies are hollow.
* Explain that on the first Easter Jesus' followers were amazed to find the tomb open and empty.
   Read Matthew 28:1–9.

FOR REFLECTION

* Which Easter custom will you adopt to help focus on the new life Christ brings to us?
* What parts of the Easter Triduum liturgy can your family attend? Participate in the dramatic Saturday night services at least once together.
* What original rituals can you think of to celebrate new life?

10

Honoring Mary
and Other Saints

The saints in heaven are like our extended family. You probably have photos of grandparents and other relatives in your house. Why not also display images of your spiritual mother and brothers and sisters in Christ? When in sight, the saints will more likely be kept in mind too. Then they can better inspire you to lead holy lives.

Honoring Mary

The Mother of God holds a special place in Catholic hearts and homes. We look to her as our model and also as our heavenly mother. To honor Mary, display her picture or statue in your home. There is a wide variety of images to choose from: Our Lady of Perpetual Help, Our Lady of Guadalupe, Our Lady of Lourdes, Our Lady of Fatima, Our Lady of Vladimir, Our Lady of the Streets, traditional Marys, icons, masterpieces of Mary, modern portrayals, and images depicting her for different races and nationalities. Some of Mary's feasts are the following:

January 1	Solemnity of Mary, Mother of God
February 2	Presentation of the Lord
March 25	Annunciation of the Lord
Saturday after the	
2nd Sunday after Pentecost	Immaculate Heart of Mary
May 31	Visitation
July 16	Our Lady of Mount Carmel
August 15	Assumption
August 22	Queenship of Mary
September 8	Birth of Mary

October 7	Our Lady of the Rosary
December 8	Immaculate Conception
December 12	Our Lady of Guadalupe
December 25	Birth of Jesus

On these days put Mary's image in a place of honor and set flowers and candles near it. Make a Mary candle, which is a large white candle marked with an M and decorated with a blue ribbon. Set in on your dining room table on Mary's feast days. During May, which is Mary's month, set up a May altar in your house using a pretty blue cloth, a candle, and fresh flowers. Crown your statue of Mary and sing or play a Marian hymn.

Teach your children not only the Hail Mary but also other favorite prayers to Mary such as the Angelus, the Memorare, and the beautiful Litany of Loreto in which we call on Mary by her titles. Pray Mary's prayer, the Magnificat. Once in a while as part of your family prayer, play or sing Marian songs.

Each day, as a family, pray together a Hail Mary or a decade of the rosary, if not an entire rosary. This might be your custom during October, the month of the Most Holy Rosary.

Introduce your children to Mary's shrines and especially the National Shrine of the Immaculate Conception in Washington. If possible, make a pilgrimage to a church or shrine named for Mary.

Give your children gifts related to Mary: a rosary, a scapular, or a medal with her image, such as the miraculous medal.

Talk about Mary, her life as in the gospels, her appearances on earth, and why we honor her.

Above all, encourage your children to imitate Mary who is the first and best disciple of Jesus. She teaches us faith, humility, and love for God and others. As a good mother, she shows us how to bring Jesus into the world.

Celebrating the Saints

One way to honor the saints is to compose a family litany of saints that includes the patron saints of every member along with some favorite saints. Pray it on special occasions.

Each year the church celebrates its members in heaven on their feast days. A saint's feast day is usually the day on which he or she died, that is, was born into eternal life. Join in some of these celebrations in the following ways:

- Attend Mass together as a family on the feast day.
- Some saints have symbols associated with them. For example, St. Andrew's is a cross in the shape of an X, while St. Maria Goretti's is a lily. For more symbols of saints see a book like *The Penguin Dictionary of Saints* by Donald Attwater with Catherine Rachel John, or a Catholic encyclopedia. Use these symbols to decorate cookies, cupcakes, cakes, balloons, placecards, napkins, or a poster or banner for the feast day.
- Display a statue or picture of the saint.
- Sing a hymn as part of the celebration.
- Plan a game related to the saint. For St. Anthony of Padua, patron of lost objects, you might have a scavenger hunt or a treasure hunt. For St. Francis of Assisi, who called his body Brother Ass, you might play Pin the Tail on the Donkey.
- Serve foods from the saint's native country.
- Be creative in devising original ways to celebrate. For example, for a feast of St. Peter, have fish for dinner.

You might adopt the following ideas for these particular feasts:

All Saints Day: November 1
Invite everyone to display statues or pictures of their patron saints and favorite saints. Give a Halloween party with games, costumes, and themes focusing on the saints. Read stories about the saints or let everyone tell about his or her saint.

St. Blaise: February 3
According to tradition, this bishop-martyr once saved the life of a boy who was choking on a fish bone. On the feast of St. Blaise, go to church to have your throats blessed. Candles in the shape of a cross are used for this, and a prayer is prayed for protection against ailments of the throat and every other illness.

St. Valentine's Day: February 14
Recall that St. Valentine was a martyr, which means that he was someone who had great love. Celebrate the day with homemade cards,
poems, and treats. Make pancakes, cakes, and cookies in the shape of
a heart. (To make a heart-shaped cake use a square pan and a circular
pan. Cut the round cake in half and place each half on adjoining sides
of the square.) As a family do an act of love for someone in need.

St. Patrick: March 17
This bishop of Ireland is known for teaching about the Trinity especially by means of the three-leafed shamrock. Wear green today.
Decorate the house and table with green. Prepare green food and bake
shamrock cookies. Say the prayer of St. Patrick known as the Lorica or
Breastplate of St. Patrick (see p. 70). Talk about the Catholic belief of
three Persons in one God.

St. Joseph: March 19
An Italian custom is to prepare a St. Joseph table. People laden a table
with food and then distribute it to the poor. Share your food with
someone today. You might also copy the custom of having cream puffs
or Italian pastries on St. Joseph's feast day. Because St. Joseph was the
breadwinner of the Holy Family, bake and serve a special bread. You
might also do something special for the father in your family.

St. Francis: October 4
This gentle saint preached love and God and peace to all. Bless your
pets today. Say the Peace Prayer (see p. 69), which is attributed to St.
Francis and begins "Lord, make me an instrument of your peace." In
the spirit of St. Francis who embraced poverty, sort through clothes
and other possessions and give extras to the poor.

St. Nicholas: December 6
St. Nicholas is the patron saint of children and presumably the origin
of our present-day Santa Claus. He was a bishop who had a heart for
the poor. According to legend, at night he secretly went to a poor man's
house and left money that could be used as a dowry for the three
daughters. On the evening of December 5, have your children put their
shoes outside their bedroom door. Fill the shoes with candy, nuts,
fruit, and small gifts.

St. Lucy: December 13

St. Lucy is an early Christian martyr. In Sweden, on the morning of her feast day, the oldest daughter wears a white dress with a red sash. On her head is a holly wreath with candles. She brings St. Lucy buns to her parents. For this day make St. Lucy buns (which are S-shaped with coiled ends) or purchase cinnamon buns.

A classic book with countless ideas for celebrating saints' feast days is *My Name Day—Come for Dessert* written by Helen McLoughlin and published by The Liturgical Press (Collegeville, MN). Although this book is out of print, you might find it in your parish library. The entire book can be found at the web site www.domestic-church.com.

Celebrating Our Uncanonized Saints

An African-American custom for deepening our understanding of our connectedness is a remembering circle. You may wish to add this ritual to your celebration of Thanksgiving, New Year's Day, Memorial Day, or All Souls Day. Set chairs in a circle. In the center place a flower or leaf arrangement and a larger candle surrounded by small vigil candles. Have your family members sit in the candlelight and think about people who have given them beautiful memories. These people may have called forth their gifts or supported them. They may be living or deceased, friends or relatives. Anyone may share a "remembering" aloud. After each one is mentioned, the group responds, "We remember you in love for these good memories." The remembering circle will make your family more aware of what it means to belong to the Communion of Saints.

Another way to remember departed loved ones is to visit the cemetery where they are buried. Clean and put flowers on their graves. Pray for them.

FOR REFLECTION

• How can your family show more devotion to the Mother of God by sacramentals? by prayer? by imitation?

• What saints could your family celebrate in a special way? How?

• How do you remember the deceased loved ones in your family?

Afterword

If you are like most parents, you have not had a course on parenting. You raise your children by what anthropologist Margaret Mead called "the sidewise look"—how others are doing it. Remembering that your sacrament of marriage provides the grace to bring up your children may encourage you. God is your invisible partner.

One way to hone your parenting skills, especially in regard to passing on the faith, is by meeting with other parents. You might organize a group of parents who are interested in nourishing the faith of their children. You can meet regularly at your parish or in a home to swap ideas and offer one another moral support. Make prayer part of the meeting. As an alternative, you might initiate the practice of inviting parents to meet informally every week after a certain Sunday liturgy. Over coffee and donuts, you could talk about ways that will help you increase faith and Catholic practice within the family. Through interaction with other members of your faith community, you will grow in confidence and faith. Together you will find new ways to make your family a little kingdom of God.

Appendix:
Some Family Prayers

Sign of the Cross
In the name of the Father, and of the Son, and of the Holy Spirit. Amen.

Apostles' Creed
I believe in God, the Father almighty, creator of heaven and earth. I believe in Jesus Christ, his only Son, our Lord. He was conceived by the power of the Holy Spirit, and born of the Virgin Mary. He suffered under Pontius Pilate, was crucified, died, and was buried. He descended to the dead. On the third day he rose again. He ascended into heaven, and is seated at the right hand of the Father. He will come again to judge the living and the dead. I believe in the Holy Spirit, the holy catholic church, the communion of saints, the forgiveness of sins, the resurrection of the body and the life everlasting. Amen.

The Lord's Prayer
Our Father, who art in heaven, hallowed be thy name; thy kingdom come, thy will be done on earth as it is in heaven. Give us this day our daily bread; and forgive us our trespasses as we forgive those who trespass against us; and lead us not into temptation, but deliver us from evil. Amen.

Hail Mary
Hail Mary, full of grace, the Lord is with you! Blessed are you among women, and blessed is the fruit of your womb, Jesus. Holy Mary, Mother of God, pray for us sinners, now, and at the hour of our death. Amen.

Doxology (Glory Be)

Glory to the Father, and to the Son, and to the Holy Spirit. As it was in the beginning, is now, and will be forever. Amen. *(new form)*

Glory be to the Father, and to the Son, and to the Holy Spirit: As it was in the beginning, is now, and ever shall be, world without end. Amen. *(traditional)*

Come, Holy Spirit

Come, Holy Spirit, fill the hearts of your faithful. And kindle in them the fire of your love. Send forth your Spirit and they shall be created. And you will renew the face of the earth.

Lord, by the light of the Holy Spirit you have taught the hearts of your faithful. In the same Spirit help us to relish what is right and always rejoice in your consolation. We ask this through Christ our Lord. Amen.

Hail, Holy Queen

Hail, holy Queen, mother of mercy, hail, our life, our sweetness, and our hope. To you we cry, poor banished children of Eve; to you we send up our sighs, mourning, and weeping in this valley of tears. Turn, then, most gracious advocate, your eyes of mercy toward us; and after this, our exile, show us the blessed fruit of your womb, Jesus; O clement, O loving, O sweet Virgin Mary.

Grace before Meals

Bless us, O Lord, and these your gifts which we are about to receive from your bounty, through Christ our Lord. Amen.

Grace after Meals

We give you thanks, almighty God, for all your gifts, who live and reign, now and forever. Amen.

Act of Contrition

My God, I am sorry for my sins with all my heart. In choosing to do wrong and failing to do good, I have sinned against you whom I should love above all things. I firmly intend, with your help, to do penance, to sin no more, and to avoid whatever leads me to sin. Our Savior Jesus Christ suffered and died for us. In his name, my God, have mercy. *(new form)*

O my God, I am heartily sorry for having offended you, and I detest all my sins, because of your just punishments, but most of all because they offend you, my God, who are all good and worthy of all my love. I firmly resolve with the help of your grace to sin no more and to avoid the near occasions of sin. *(traditional)*

Morning Offering

O Jesus, through the Immaculate Heart of Mary, I offer you all of my prayers, works, joys, and sufferings of this day in union with the Holy Sacrifice of the Mass throughout the world. I offer them for all the intentions of your Sacred Heart: the salvation of souls, reparation for sin, the reunion of all Christians. I offer them for the intentions of our bishops, and of all Apostles of Prayer, and in particular for those recommended by our Holy Father this month. Amen.

The Jesus Prayer

Lord Jesus Christ, Son of God, have mercy on me, a sinner.

Act of Faith

O my God, I firmly believe that you are one God in three divine Persons, Father, Son, and Holy Spirit; I believe that your divine Son became man and died for our sins, and that he will come to judge the living and the dead. I believe these and all the truths which the Holy Catholic Church teaches, because you revealed them, who can neither deceive nor be deceived. Amen.

Act of Hope

O my God, relying on your infinite goodness and promises, I hope to obtain pardon of my sins, the help of your grace, and life everlasting, through the merits of Jesus Christ, my Lord and Redeemer. Amen.

Act of Love

O my God, I love you above all things, with my whole heart and soul, because you are all good and worthy of all my love. I love my neighbor as myself for the love of you. I forgive all who have injured me, and I ask pardon of all whom I have injured. Amen.

Memorare

Remember, O most gracious virgin Mary, that never was it known that anyone who fled to your protection, implored your help, or sought your intercession was left unaided. Inspired by this confidence, I fly to you, O virgin of virgins, my Mother. To you I come, before you I stand sinful and sorrowful. O Mother of the Word Incarnate, despise not my petitions, but in your mercy, hear and answer me. Amen.

The Angelus

V. The angel of the Lord declared unto Mary
R. And she conceived of the Holy Spirit.
Hail, Mary...

V. Behold the handmaid of the Lord.
R. Be it done to me according to your word.
Hail, Mary...

V. And the Word was made flesh
R. And dwelt among us.
Hail, Mary...

V. Pray for us, O holy Mother of God,
R. That we may be made worthy of the promises of Christ.

Let us pray.
Pour forth, we beseech you, O Lord, your grace into our hearts: that we, to whom the incarnation of Christ, your son, was made known by the message of an angel, may by his passion and cross be brought to the glory of his resurrection. Through the same Christ our Lord. Amen.

Queen of Heaven

Queen of Heaven, rejoice, alleluia:
For he whom you merited to bear, alleluia,
Has risen as he said, alleluia.
Pray for us to God, alleluia.

V. Rejoice and be glad, O Virgin Mary, alleluia.
R. Because the Lord is truly risen. Alleluia.

Let us pray.
O God, who by the resurrection of your son, our Lord Jesus Christ, granted joy to the whole world: grant we beg you, that through the intercession of the Virgin Mary, his mother, we may attain the joys of eternal life. Through the same Christ our Lord. Amen.

The Rosary

Begin by praying the Apostles' Creed on the crucifix followed by an Our Father, three Hail Marys, and a Glory Be on the introductory chain. Then for each decade of the circle, pray an Our Father, ten Hail Marys, and close with a Glory Be. While praying the words, reflect on one set of mysteries, one mystery for each decade.

Joyful Mysteries
1. The Annunciation
2. The Visitation
3. The Birth of Jesus
4. The Presentation
5. The Finding of Jesus in the Temple

Sorrowful Mysteries
1. The Agony in the Garden
2. The Scourging at the Pillar
3. The Crowning with Thorns
4. The Carrying of the Cross
5. The Crucifixion

Glorious Mysteries
1. The Resurrection
2. The Ascension
3. The Descent of the Holy Spirit
4. The Assumption of Mary
5. The Crowning of Mary as Queen of Heaven and Earth

Prayer for the Dead
Eternal rest grant to him (her), O Lord, and let perpetual light shine upon him (her). May his (her) soul and the souls of all the faithful departed, through the mercy of God, rest in peace. Amen.

Prayers to the Guardian Angel
Angel sent by God to guide me,
be my light and walk beside me;
be my guardian and protect me;
on the paths of life direct me. Amen. *(new form)*

Angel of God, my guardian dear,
to whom God's love commits me here.
Ever this day be at my side
to light and to guard,
to rule and to guide. Amen. *(traditional)*

Prayer to Saint Michael
Saint Michael the Archangel, defend us in battle; be our protection against the wickedness and snares of the devil. May God rebuke him, we humbly pray; and do you, O prince of the heavenly host, by the power of God, thrust into hell Satan and all other evil spirits who prowl through the world seeking the ruin of souls. Amen.

Soul of Christ
Soul of Christ, sanctify me.
Body of Christ, save me.
Blood of Christ, inebriate me.
Water from the side of Christ, wash me.

Passion of Christ, strengthen me.

O good Jesus, hear me.
Within your wounds shelter me.
Never permit me to be separated from you.
From the evil one protect me.
At the hour of my death call me and bid me come to you,
that I may praise you with all your saints forever and ever. Amen.

The Way of the Cross
   I.   Jesus is condemned to death on the cross.
   II.   Jesus accepts his cross.
   III.   Jesus falls the first time.
   IV.   Jesus meets his sorrowful mother.
   V.   Simon of Cyrene helps Jesus carry his cross.
   VI.   Veronica wipes the face of Jesus.
   VII.   Jesus falls the second time.
   VIII.   Jesus meets and speaks to the women of Jerusalem.
   IX.   Jesus falls the third time.
   X.   Jesus is stripped of his garments.
   XI.   Jesus is nailed to the cross.
   XII.   Jesus dies on the cross.
   XIII.   Jesus is taken down from the cross and laid in his mother's arms.
   XIV.   Jesus is placed in the tomb.
   XV.   Jesus rises from the dead.

Take, O Lord, and Receive
Take, O Lord, and receive all my liberty, my memory, my understanding, and my entire will. Whatever I have and possess you have given all to me. To you, Lord, I now return it. All is yours. Dispose of it according to your will. Give me only your love and your grace; with these I will be rich enough and desire nothing more.

Prayer for Peace
Lord, make me an instrument of your peace;
where there is hatred, let me sow love;

where there is injury, pardon;
where there is doubt, faith;
where there is despair, hope
where there is darkness, light;
where there is sadness, joy.

Grant that I may not so much seek
to be consoled, as to console,
to be understood, as to understand;
to be loved as to love;
for it is in giving that we receive,
it is in pardoning that we are pardoned;
and it is in dying that we are born to eternal life.

St. Patrick's Breastplate

Christ with me, Christ before me, Christ behind me,
Christ within me, Christ beneath me, Christ above me,
Christ on my right, Christ on my left,
Christ where I lie, Christ where I sit, Christ where I arise,
Christ in the heart of everyone who thinks of me,
Christ in the mouth of everyone who speaks of me,
Christ in every eye that sees me,
Christ in every ear that hears me.

St. Richard of Chichester

Thank you, Lord Jesus Christ, for all the benefits and blessings you have given me, for all the pains you have borne for me. Merciful Friend, Brother, and Redeemer, may I know you more clearly, love you more dearly, and follow you more nearly, day by day.

Pope John Paul II's Prayer for Families

Lord God, from you every family in heaven and on earth takes its name. Father, you are love and life. Through your Son, Jesus Christ, born of woman, and through the Holy Spirit, fountain of Divine Charity, grant that each family on earth may become for each successive generation a true shrine of life and love.

Grant that your grace may guide the thoughts and actions of husbands and wives for the good of their families and of all the families in the world. Grant that the young may find in the family solid support for their human dignity and for their growth in truth and love. Grant that love, strengthened by the grace of the sacrament of marriage, may prove mightier than all the weaknesses and trials through which our families sometimes pass.

Through the intercession of the Holy Family of Nazareth, grant that the church may fruitfully carry out her worldwide mission in the family and through the family. Through Christ our Lord who is the Way, the Truth and the Life forever and ever. Amen.

Also by Sr. Mary Kathleen...

The Bible Way to Prayer
God's 800 Number for Everyone

Provides reflective and concrete means for savoring God's love, for encountering God through Scripture and for delving into the richness of God's Word. Some topics covered are personalizing the Bible, using the *lectio divina* method of meditation, using variations of the psalms and other biblical prayers.

1-58595-108-0, 104 pp, $9.95 (J-69)

Prayer-Moments for Every Day of the Year

A wonderful collection of one sentence prayers, organized into categories. Drawing from the Bible, the saints, and the liturgy, the author packs a treasure chest of short prayers for every need, for every expression of human emotion and of divine love.

0-89622-748-0, 80 pp, $7.95 (B-82)

Discipline Made Easy
Positive Tips & Techniques for Religion Teachers

Hundreds of tried and true ways to achieve discipline in religion class.

0-89622-598-4, 112 pp, $7.95 (W-46)

Saints for Children
Stories, Activities, Prayer Services

Features 12 popular saints. Emphasizes each saint's virtues and how middle graders can practice these virtues in their lives. Includes an account of the saint's life and good works, a prayer service, discussion questions, activities, and games.

0-89622-738-3, 80 pp, $9.95 (B-40)

Available at religious bookstores or from:

TWENTY-THIRD PUBLICATIONS

PO BOX 180 · 185 WILLOW STREET MYSTIC, CT 06355 · 1-800-321-0411
FAX: 1-800-572-0788 BAYARD E-MAIL: ttpubs@aol.com

Call for a free catalog